HOW TC

YOUR WIFE HAPPY

AND LOVE YOU

MORE

A Practical Guide To Becoming The Dream Husband
To Your Wife Even If She's Fallen Out Of Love With
You; Save Your Relationship, Increase Satisfaction,
And Have A Lasting Marriage Without Fears Or
Threats Of Divorce

William Foltz

William Foltz

How To Make Your Wife Happy And Love You More

INTRODUCTION

Your wife is another you. The earlier you accept this hard fact, the better for you. Since you married her into your home, you've become one flesh and body. This means that you are, under the marriage vow, inseparable and more vital. But it doesn't just stop there; marriage, as you know, is for better or worse. Even though there may be ups and downs in the process, what is necessary is to sustain the promise you made to each other – to love and live in harmony with one another forever.

Your wife is your "perfect" partner, and since you are her spouse forever, it's wise to ensure your relationship is a blissful one. Cheerful relationships start with excellent communication and an eagerness to hear each other out and keep the happiness and enthusiasm flowing.

The best way to enjoy a happy and flourishing marriage is to keep up with the euphoria and bliss in such a relationship. Regardless of what difficulties are tossed into your lives as a couple, you need to keep the fire of happiness and laughter in your marriage burning.

How To Make Your Wife Happy And Love You More

In this book, we shall discuss in practical terms how you could encourage your wife by always making her happy, even when she does not deserve it. The idea is that when both of you turn out blissful, the relationship prospers significantly more. That is how it works, and this is why you should be familiar with the techniques or ways of doing that.

Beyond making your spouse continuously pleased, you will also familiarize yourself with the powerful tools for effective communication in marriage as well as the untold acts that are capable of destroying marriages. The essence of all this is to make you understand better why you should make your marriage a blissful one devoid of threats of separation or divorce.

William Foltz

CHAPTER 1

Practical Ways To Make Your Wife Happy

1. Make yourself a blissful individual

The initial step to fulfilling your desire to make your wife happy is to create bliss inside yourself. You can't make your wife comfortable on the off chance you couldn't satisfy yourself. Hence, figure out how to be a carefree individual. Be a more sure and proactive individual. Conquer the relics of days gone that make you a miserable individual, similar to your previous slip-ups. Embrace your spouse with bliss and inspiration, not with bitterness and pessimism.

2. Set up her morning meal

Setting someone up for a morning meal or breakfast entails sacrificing your time by waking up at dawn. In the event that you rise early and set up a sound and scrumptious breakfast for your significant other, she will clearly feel honored and blissful. If you don't have the foggiest idea about cooking, then begin figuring out how. The Web is loaded with recipes and video instructional exercises.

3. Give her a cheerful environment

Continuously be aware of your partner's current circumstances. Is it getting exhausting or bleak? Why not play cool and cheerful melodies to light up her day? Is your home or room chaotic and filthy? Why not tidy it up and make it comfortable? Do individuals around her make her miserable and focused? Why not carry her to an ocean side or any spot that will help her unwind and relax?

4. Tell her how lovely she is

We won't wed our own significant other in the event that we were not struck by their appeal and excellence. Continuously remind you're her how wonderful she is. Continuously remind her how ideal that piece of her body draws in you most. What's more, obviously, don't take a gander at different ladies like an eager wolf. Keep your eyes just on your wonderful spouse.

5. Try not to deceive her

Satisfy your words and commitments. Give her what you have guaranteed, whether it's a basic gift, the time you two consented to meet in a specific spot, or the commitment you've made to improve yourself. Never break your significant other's confidence in you.

6. Be faithful to her

Your wife will be genuinely happy, assuming she will be sure that she is your only one. Thus never at any point cheat or even endeavor to make it happen. Try not to offer Satan a chance to entice you and obliterate your marriage. Give your better half absolute reliability so she won't ever be shaky or envious of some other lady.

7. Believe her

It's terrible to be blamed for cheating, being a terrible lady, being a flippant individual, a liar, or some other misleading charges, particularly in the event that there is no proof. Assuming that you do this to your spouse, it will disappoint her and even torment her brain.

To satisfy her effectively, show her that you trust her. Cause her to feel that she is trusted. Reality will become unavoidable. However long you have no evidence that she is lying or can't be relied upon, don't quit trusting and adoring her. Recall that you won't acquire stress and feel a little unsure.

Misleading questions and presumptions make superfluous boundaries in a relationship. Try not to make flippant claims when you have no proof to demonstrate them. Scrutinizing her pointlessly or checking her ow, things will baffle her. All things being equal, trust her and cause her to feel esteemed.

8. Give her all your cash

Giving up the entirety of your well deserved pay and cash fulfills your significant other for some reasons. One explanation is that it shows that you trust her. Another explanation is that it gives her the affirmation that you are just spending your cash on her and your kids, not on different ladies and different things past her insight.

9. Figure out how to cherish and deal with yourself

Your significant other's obligation isn't just to deal with your children yet in addition to dealing with you. She is continuously seeking divine intervention that her husband will be solid and well. Suppose you are that sort of spouse who is continuously drinking liquor, smoking, and pigging out on unfortunate food varieties. Most certainly, your significant other will be miserable.

To make her feel excited all the time, begin adoring and dealing with yourself. Stop your indecencies that are making your body and soul powerless. Continuously take care when you travel. Try not to be a hot-tempered individual who generally enjoys battling with outsiders. Quit making your wife stressed! Give her inner serenity.

10. Excuse her
Try not to be cruel on your wife. Excuse her in the event that she has committed errors, particularly assuming she is earnestly requesting your absolution. On the off chance that it's simply little slip-ups or negligible things, excuse her even before she lets you know she is grieved. Recall that when there is no contempt and hatred in your heart, you won't stir up some dust to disturb the great energies in your relationship.

11. Be modest and concede your own errors
Try not to fault your better half for your own errors. Also, don't do stupid things to cause her to feel regretful just to accuse her. Be a genuine man by conceding your own missteps. Be unassuming and apologize earnestly. Assuming you will show lowliness, your wife will definitely encounter felicity.

12. Cause her to feel esteemed and appreciated
Being a responsible wife is never an easy task, let alone becoming a capable mother and light of your household. Maybe, your wife is unemployed and she just stays full

time at home. Yet, recollect that being a housewife is an incredible work on its own, and dealing with your home, your kids and you is a ton of work.

Therefore, cause her to feel how significant she is that your life relies upon her. Value all that she accomplishes for yourself as well as your youngsters. Give her irregular gifts and thank you messages to make her grin following a tiring day.

13. Regard her

Try not to cause her to feel that she is losing herself. Regard her uniqueness personally and as a lady. Try not to compel her to play billiard and stop her to play badminton assuming her energy is the last option. Try not to drive her to watch Vindicators and deny her of watching the Notepad on the off chance that she prefers heartfelt than dream films. Also, don't force her to engage in sexual relations in the event that she's stressed up and could not do it right now.

14. Honor her

Honor your better half. Suppose you're a boozer or a sluggish spouse. Suppose you are a miscreant? Suppose you are a flighty dad to your kids. What do you expect your wife to say to her companions and family members? Try not to disgrace her yet; cause her to feel honored to have you as her better half and a dad to her kids.

Be a dependable spouse by giving your wife her necessities, like cash, care, love, fondness, trust, and understanding. Be a responsible dad to your children by being a good example and working harder to fabricate a more promising time to come for them.

15. Love and regard her loved ones
Your spouse will not be blissful assuming you have clashes with her folks and kin. Subsequently, give your all to win the core of your better half as well as win the hearts of her loved ones. However you and your better half are now living respectively in a different house from her folks; remember to visit them consistently to lay out an amicable relationship with them. Cause them to feel that their family is developing greater, not contracting and blurring.

16. Love her through various challenges
To wrap things up, satisfy your marriage promise to her and save it forever. Continuously accompany her through various challenges, in affliction and wellbeing, and in

inconveniences and festivities. Try not to leave her for another lady since she isn't now fulfilling you in bed. Try not to consider it a quit in light of the fact that your family is now monetarily broke.

Anything the issue is, you and your spouse ought to continuously be an incredible group to defeat any issues and difficulties. Make her really cheerful by tracking down bliss in rehearsing persistence in the midst of every marital issue.

17. Give her your audience and attention

Most men's thought process is they need to ascend the mountains or do something uncommon to satisfy their spouses. Your wife is someone very much like you and people have feelings. Now and then when she has an unpleasant day, all she needs is somebody to pay attention to her persistently. Be her audience, don't pass judgment, and allow her to loosen up by confiding in you. Try not to attempt to give ideas or fix her concerns. Keep your open ears and simply tune in. What's more, when she's finished, give her a major embrace to encourage her. This is additionally how to make your wife happy when she becomes irate or desolate.

Some of the time, when she shares an idea with you, she isn't anticipating an answer. She basically needs to loosen up. You should simply pay attention to her without judgment, embrace her, and let her know you're there for her.

18. Embrace her ordinary

At the point when you leave or get back after working all day, make it your main goal to embrace her. Perhaps include a kiss and you have a triumphant reward not too far off. Normal substantial contact is the foundation of enduring and satisfying heartfelt relationships. Recall that often.

19. Praise her in open at whatever point you present

In the event that you're considering acquainting your better half with your companions, collaborators, or some other groups of friends, make sure you do that with a commendation. It very well might be a little accomplishment for you; however it makes a big difference to your spouse. A commendation out in the public demonstrates that you recognize her as your wife and as well depicts the way you treasure your relationship with her. Do this on the off chance that you're serious about satisfying her consistently.

20. Do a few errands for her

Whether it's making the bed or doing the clothing, doing a couple of family errands for her will reflect the amount you care, causing your home genuinely to feel like a dwelling place for both of you.

21. Cook for her

Making a hand crafted meal for your wife is one of the most outstanding ways of prevailing upon her. Continuously ask what she needs to eat. It's tied in with being her own slave yet rather focusing on her necessities. What's more, when you cook her favorite food, she'll be frantically infatuated with you regarding that.

This is an attempted and tried method for causing her to feel happy and exceptional. You can make her a heartfelt feast or a straightforward dish she cherishes. Your endeavors and signals will count more than the taste!

22. Treat Her with consideration, empathy and effortlessness

Never take a brutal tone or be critical with regards to conversing with your spouse and listening to her. Be caring, act with effortlessness, and talk in a delicate tone. This guarantees that you don't put on a show of being an undermining individual yet rather somebody she can trust and open up to.

Try not to utilize an unforgiving tone or horrible and critical language. Your consideration will make it simpler for her to talk to you openly. Additionally, be courageous (open entryways for her or pull up her seat) and be obliging of her time and responsibilities.

23. Praise her looks

Make sure to commend her looks occasionally. This goes quite far and keeps the happiness overflowing. Assuming she requests your perspective on the thing she's wearing, give thoughtfulness regarding the colors and designs and appreciate her choices. On the off chance that you could do without it, simply advise her to attempt another outfit; however never under any circumstance say that the dress looks horrible on her.

Also, offering praises is an incredible method for supporting certainty. Praise her on her accomplishments, looks, abilities, and all that makes her exceptional. Do it when alone as well as when you are before partners, companions, and family members. It will show her that you won't hesitate to tell others the amount you love her.

24. Shock her generally

She's your better half and she merits the best. So shock her by taking her out on intriguing visits and events a couple of times each year. Make sure to put something aside for these events and when you do celebrate, do it with style. Give her choices to look over and ask her where she needs to go.

Likewise, you don't have to trust that your commemoration will astound her with gifts. She will be thrilled to get shocks from you, regardless of whether they are not costly. Gift her something fun, eccentric, or helpful - you'd know best what to get her!

25. Help her out

In the event that your significant other is aggressive or attempting to maintain another business or begin a genuinely new thing – help her out. Try not to scrutinize and be the mainstay of help she wants. Pay attention to her cautiously and consistently view what she says in a serious way. Regard her decisions and never judge them. In some cases you may not concur with what she's doing yet don't rush in and belittle her. Be quiet, remain attentive, and help her fill in the holes.

26. Acknowledge her for what her identity is

Nobody's perfect; everyone commits errors and it's a fundamental piece of being human. Your wife might leave the shower taps on, neglect to turn off the microwave or do senseless things around the house could upset you. Perhaps she does that unexpectedly or is a piece careless, yet you shouldn't upbraid her for it. Unobtrusively seal up or deal with the disasters and acknowledge those easily overlooked details as being essential for her. Likewise, getting pushed or furious over such little things isn't worth the effort.

27. Try not to underestimate her

Marriage is a framework and in some cases we lost all sense of direction in it. It's critical to not deal with your better half like a house robot that essentially finishes tasks, takes care of the children, and so on. Never underestimate her yet all things being equal, deal with her like a sweetheart. Go out on dates with her and invest energy like how you'd typically enjoy when you initially entered a relationship with her prior to choosing to get hitched.

28. Go to battle for her

Suppose you and your significant other go out together and somebody ridicules her. This is the time you don't simply leave with her; you rather stand up and fight for her. Regardless of whether it implies seriously jeopardizing yourself, it shows that you're willing to commit your life to her and safeguard her. Ladies once in a while feel helpless and this is the point at which it really depends on men to secure and really focus on them.

29. Show your affection to her

Telling her regularly that you love her, sending her hello cards, roses, and chocolates on your commemorations and birthday events – these things make a big difference to ladies. Furthermore, don't simply say it, show it too. Get to know each other alone during the evening and flash up the sentiment. Try not to disregard her affection or feelings and consistently give her physical and profound love.

30. Be thankful to her

Be thankful to your wife and always offer your thanks. Tell her you love her frequently and how your entire world has improved since the day she entered your life. You can make this a stride further by giving her unexpected gifts. Help her seek after her fantasies and forever show up for her, at whatever point she really wants you.

31. Dedicate your time

In the event that you haven't been giving her time, space, or truly – your part of the arrangement when the opportunity arrives, then, at that point, it's about time you made it up to her. Apologize, and make your later opportunity together way more important. Take her out for candlelight suppers, films, shopping, or even to visits in historical centers and craftsmanship studios. Become familiar with another expertise together and enjoy leisure activities. Lose yourselves in the fun together and simply make every moment count.

32. Understand what she needs/loves

Focus on her preferences – breakfast in bed, blossoms, dessert by the day's end, paying attention to a specific tune to unwind, or some espresso at night. Or on the other hand perhaps she simply maintains that you should put the latrine seat down or hang your towel. Doing such little demonstrations can likewise cause her to feel like you figure her out.

33. Groom yourself

Do you focus on your appearance now as you did before marriage? On the off chance that you don't, you ought to invest a little energy on yourself and intrigue her with your prepped appearance and some great scent. Tell her that she is as yet worth dazzling.

34. Plan heartfelt dates and lengthy drives

You may not understand it, yet your better half invests the vast majority of her energy shuffling among family and work responsibilities. Offer her a genuinely necessary reprieve by arranging a heartfelt date or a lengthy drive involving both of you only. This will likewise give you an opportunity to associate. You can likewise engage in outside exercises that you love doing together.

35. Get her blossoms

This good thought is a long way from banality and will, without a doubt, be valued by her. Be that as it may, you really want not to sit tight for a unique event. All things being equal, out of nowhere, shock her with a bouquet or a solitary rose.

36. Settle on her a piece of your choices

Your wife is your partner in all things; cause her to have that impression. Include her in choices connected with the family and funds. Cause her to feel included and esteemed in the choices. Ask her for her perspective, even in the little things, rather than keeping her out of the loop.

37. Give her space

Very much like you, your significant other additionally needs her "personal" time or individual space. So when you notice that she is worn out and needs to unwind, give her space. Assume control over the entirety of her family obligations and urge her to loosen up with a day at a spa or by meeting her companions.

38. Be sexy and energetic

Sexual association assumes a significant part in any relationship or marriage. Be lively and attempt new things to energize your spouse. Physical contacts like kisses, embraces, and snuggling can cause her to feel appealing and cherished. Try not to stay away, and keep your game up.

All in all, you might have heard the well known maxim that "a cheerful spouse is a blissful life". Since this statement contains some reality, men frequently search for fascinating plans to satisfy their spouses. Your words and signals will frequently accomplish beyond what costly gifts can. Seeing and valuing little subtleties, embracing her frequently, confiding in her, and being thoughtful can go far in keeping your wife happy and feeling esteemed. In this way, the following time you need to carry a grin to her face, basically say thanks to her for all she accomplishes for you.

CHAPTER 2

Most Ideal Ways To Romance Your Wife

After a significant stretch of time, the enthusiasm in a marriage can start to blur. Keep the fire bursting at the seams with these effective methods for romancing your better half. They include:

1. Date your significant other

On the off chance that you asked her out again today, could she actually be eager to say OK? You have probably been very great at this at one time or she could not have possibly hitched you! So why stop now? One date a month at least. Utilize your creative mind, get inventive, and make it extraordinary.

2. Cause her to feel unique (don't underestimate the relationship).

On the off chance that you haven't effectively exhibited how exceptional she is in the past four hours, then, you've wasted too much time to do that. This is certainly not a high financial plan thing; it's a high thought thing. When last did you give her an "I love you call" or offer her flowers at her office? Do you actually open the vehicle entryway? Serve her hot tea, wash her vehicle, convey a surprising hug, a foot rub, or candles with supper? You understand.

3. Utilize some creative mind.
Plan occasions, dates, nights at home or outings with the sort of imaginative reasoning that propelled you when you previously asked her out. This is time to activate such thoughts and creative mindset again to make her happy and flourishing.

4. Deal with yourself
Take time off and ponder how you dress around your wife, discard the cigarettes, begin some standard activity; don't be a lazy pig. When she sees you, does she require another glance – or does she turn away? Does the manner in which you introduce yourself tell her you believe she should be drawn to you or do you underestimate all that?

5. Tell her "I love you" and say it frequently
How frequently do you let your spouse know that you love her? Regardless of whether she realizes that you do, there is no damage in communicating it as frequently as possible. Obviously, you could likewise say these words with little motions.

6. Be caring

Be caring and generous to her. This is usually underplayed, underestimated, misjudged, and absolutely underutilized, but it works. Do you want your wife to be romantic? Be Mr. Generosity. Figure out how to make mindfulness and thoughts your second nature. Pleasant folks truly do finish first and she'll succumb to you once more.

7. Be a man of his word

Keep in mind, honorable men are obliging, conscious, polite, dependable, liberal, unassuming, and enchanting Stand up when she leaves the table, open the vehicle entryway, stroll on the road side of the walkway. Help her on with her coat; hurry to the vehicle for her umbrella… you understand everything.

8. Tell her she's lovely

Ladies who hear their spouse let them know they're delightful become more gorgeous. Men who tell their spouses they're wonderful accept it with more conviction each time the words leave their lips. It's a shared benefit. It doesn't damage to uphold your words. Just tell her often how cute and lovely she's become.

9. Hang out

How To Make Your Wife Happy And Love You More

There are just 168 hours in every week – the number won't ever differ. How much time we offer our relationships can seem like a vote with regards to the amount we value individuals we say we love. Romance like anything more advantageous merits the speculation of time and consideration. Continuously guarantee that you know the various meanings of romantic expressions that you and your better half have and use often.

How To Make Your Angry Wife Happy and Forgive You

Ladies can be capricious. They can lash out at you without leaving any hint. Also, when you attempt to converse with them, they will stay away from you and overlook your expectation to know what's the deal with them. Assuming your better half is that way, you need to effectively encourage her and make her excuse you for any error you have committed.

Recollect that the joy of your wife is fundamental for the sound and merry presence of your marriage. She likewise fills in as the radiance of your home. Without euphoria in her heart, your home could be melancholy. Thus, on the off chance that you love your spouse, assuming you esteem your marriage and you care for your family, you must be patient and have the guts to reestablish and keep up with her bliss.

The following are the different ways you can make her cheerful and pardon you:

1. Show lowliness

Your pride and self image will just make your woman angrier. Consequently, be unassuming. Be practical so you can lift and hoist her degree of joy. Assuming you exhibit humility, it will be simpler for you to follow the subsequent stages underneath.

2. Understand your misstep

At the point when your better half is distraught, don't respond with one or more franticness of yours. It will just muddle things. All things considered, be proactive and ponder yourself to figure out your flaws. Then, at that point, with your lowliness, concede your mix-ups.

3. Apologize genuinely

Tell her how sorry you are. Show that you are earnest and you think about your mix-up as something serious. Ridiculing your error or her inclination, and trifling with it will just exasperate her anger towards you. In this manner, don't quit saying 'sorry' and be reliable with your earnestness.

4. Pay attention to her grumbling

Allow her to converse with you and release her complaints. Cause her to feel that it's OK to be transparent about what she genuinely feels.

5. Give her an opportunity

If you notice that your significant other doesn't have any desire to converse with you or even see your face, give her sufficient opportunity and space until she needs to. Most ladies need to invest more energy alone to silent themselves when they are furious. Regard their "personal" time.

6. Assure her that you will not rehash a similar error

Assuming she is irate on the grounds that you have pursued a major choice without her assent, give her a confirmation that it won't ever occur from this point forward. Give her certainty by turning out to be more open to your significant other. Share your arrangements to her and ask her assent when you simply decide, whether they are huge or little.

7. Be humane

Show sympathy. Feel her anguish. Cause her to feel that you can likewise sympathize with her aggravation. Show her that you comprehend what she has been going through and you are effectively taking care of her concerns, not aggravate them.

8. Charm her

Assuming that she is distraught on the grounds that you have made her extremely upset, let her wrecked heart recuperate and make it lively again by charming her. Give her roses, give her a piece of gems, send her an affection letter, treat her to a heartfelt supper, or simply cook her favorite dinner. Do all you can to prevail upon her very much like what you did when she previously experienced passionate feelings for you.

9. Give her something she has been yearning to have

Make her blissful and fail to remember her hatred by making one of her fantasies materialize. Could it be said that she is longing for an excursion in a delightful ocean side hotel? Is it safe to say that she is yearning to purchase that exquisite and polished dress you both saw in a store? Effectively make her fantasies a reality.

10. Show her that you are working harder to be a superior man

Maybe she is irate on the grounds that she is now burnt out on you. Her understanding is now missing the mark since you don't improve. Satisfy her again by showing her that you are putting forth a valiant effort to be a superior individual. Give her expectation by beginning to get out from under your vices. In any case, basically show her that you are advancing and pushing ahead.

11. Be more joyful and really sympathetic

Joyfulness and happiness are "infectious". For instance, In the event that you are a positive and happy individual, your wife could continuously snicker and grin at you. Yet, assuming you are dependably miserable and disturbed, she could become irritated, lose trust, confidence, and joy in you. She could be tainted with your irritation and may become miserable as well. Besides, in the event that you are a generous individual, it will be simpler for her to pardon you as well. Nonetheless, assuming that you're brutal with your wife, she could likewise be unforgiving with you.

Satisfy her by creating more joy inside you. At the end of the day, be a happy individual so you could impact more satisfaction in her. Be cheerful and content throughout everyday life. Figure out how to love straightforward things with your spouse. Be a good example of euphoria and joy. Besides, figure out how to pardon her, as well as yourself. At the point when you are a generous individual, she won't find it hard to pardon you as well.

12. Cause her to feel the amount you love her

Ladies can be desirous and unreliable. They may likewise feel powerless. Those sentiments can make them miserable, depleted, and angry. If you have any desire to make your wife extremely happy and pardon you, show that you are dedicated to her. Give her certainty that she's the one to focus on. What's more, above all, adore her often. Love her by paying attention to her, giving her requirements, and following her needs, particularly assuming they will make your marriage more joyful, better, and last longer.

So have you at any point accomplished something that made your spouse frantic at you? How did you make her grin once more and pardon you? What procedures did you use to reestablish the harmony and bliss in your marriage? Reflect on what you have just read on this section and put them into practice.

How To Make Your Wife Happy And Love You More

CHAPTER 3

Powerful Tools For Effective Communication In Marriage

Improving communication skills is very necessary for a healthy and lasting marriage. This is because communication is the bedrock for every successful relationship and as thus, couples need to communicate effectively in order to understand themselves better and be in a better position to enjoy increasing marital satisfaction. Therefore, the keys to effective communication in marriage include the following:

1. Be deliberate about spending time together

Couples frequently invest almost no energy in significant discussion consistently. To change this, switch off the gadgets and make it a must to spend at least 30 minutes together every day. This will help you to know and understand each other better.

2. Utilize more "I" explanations and less "You" statements

This diminishes the possibilities of your life partner feeling like they need to safeguard themselves. For

instance, "I wish you would recognize more frequently
how much work I do at home to deal with you and the
kids."

3. Be explicit
At the point when issues emerge, be explicit. Wide
speculations as, "You do it constantly!" are not useful.

4. Stay away from mind-perusing
It is extremely baffling when another person behaves like
they understand better compared to you what you were
truly thinking.

5. Try not to anticipate that they should guess what you might be thinking too
This is quite possibly one of the most well-known
botches in marriage and relationships. They expect the
other individual in the situation to guess what they might
be thinking, which is simply impractical.

Despite how long and how well somebody has known
you, they can't guess what you might be thinking.
Expecting that from them can prompt unfortunate and
weak communication.

6. Be constructive in expressing negative feelings

There will be times when you feel harshness, disdain, dissatisfaction or objection. You need to register these feelings for change to happen. Be that as it may, how you offer these viewpoints is basic. You should express such negative thoughts in a cautious and polite manner.

7. Listen to her without being defensive

For a union to flourish, the two couples should have the option to hear each other's protests without getting guarded. This is a lot harder than figuring out how to successfully communicate negative thoughts.

8. Unreservedly express good feelings

A great many people are quicker to communicate ill feelings than positive ones. It is essential to the strength of your marriage that you affirm your partner. Always express positive feelings in the form of appreciation, fondness, regard, profound respect, endorsement, etc. Assuming that your commendations surpass your objections, your wife will focus on your complaints. On the off chance that your objections surpass your commendations, your analysis will fail to receive any notice.

9. Engage in face-to-face conversation every day

You will frequently observe that you're depleted in the wake of adjusting every one of your obligations toward the day's end. When you arrive at home, you are depleted to such an extent that the sum of everything on your mind is simply investing energy loosening up in your own space and with your viewpoints.

This doesn't allow for yourself as well as your companion to reconnect or get to know one another. However it might appear as though an errand from the get go, you should save only a couple of moments to talk up close and personal with each other. You will before long come to cherish and value this face-to-face interaction, for it provides you with an incredible approach to reconnecting.

The way to understand how to further develop communication in a marriage is to put it shortly with one another, away from all the other things.

Regardless of whether it's right before you head to sleep around evening time, be certain that you talk with each other about absolutely everything and perceive how this truly assists with opening the conduits and get you two talking once more.

10. Set aside a few minutes for just both of you (like night out)

Having that time every day assists you with recalling what you love about one another. This definitely prompts the requirement for having additional time committed to only you two.

Regardless of whether you can get a night out on the town one time per month, let it all out — this can be the life saver of your marriage and keep the communication fit as a fiddle.

Having time away from the children, away from obligations, and zeroed in on you as a couple truly makes you more grounded. This offers you a brilliant chance for good discussion and reconnecting, which is what effective communication is actually about over the long haul.

11. Discuss something other than the usual

It's not difficult to get involved in talking about tidying the house or getting the children each and every day. This will imply that your communication is substantially more about the commonplace and considerably less about the great discussion that keeps you connected together.

Make it a must to discuss the things you like, leisure activities, exceptional interests, recent developments, or something besides the utilitarian, for it will keep the flash alive and guarantee that you appreciate conversing with one another.

Further developing effective communication in marriage requires you and your companion to attempt various subjects and roads for keeping things energizing and away from the dull and ordinary.

12. Be a veritable and humble listener

One of the fundamental ways of further developing communication with your life partner is to set to the side your inner self and venture out towards being available to tuning in. Being a humble and great listener would likewise welcome a similar propensity in your spouse.

To be a great listener, you can attempt the following:

(i)   Eliminate any interruptions – like your telephones or other gadgets.

(ii)   Watch for non-verbal prompts and signals.

(iii) Show interest, identify or sympathize with her if need be.

(iv)   You can ask questions but avoid unnecessary interruptions

(v)   In particular, think before you talk.

Keep in mind – regardless of how difficult it could appear, being truly intrigued by your companion is totally your decision.

13. Shift focus over to one another for help

You need to help one another, and you need to be the one individual that your life partner can go to. The best way to arrive is through effective communication in a marriage.

Realize that a decent marriage vigorously relies on love and support, and when you confide in one another along these lines, you assist with cultivating one of the fundamental components of being a lovely couple — the spouses who support each other will continuously remain close and steadfast in their marriage!

14. Your tone matters a lot to her

At the point when we attempt to speak with somebody, it isn't just about the words we use, yet in addition the tone we express those words in. How do you develop effective communication in marriage through tone? Assuming you and your wife talk in a tone that is hostile or provoking, it can prompt a contention among you, making communication significantly more troublesome. A happy and cheerful tone could do better.

15. Focus on your body language as well

Very much like your tone, your body language is additionally a non-verbal communication approach you need to utilize for effective communication in your marriage. On the off chance that you seem to be cautious, insulted, or furious and fomented by your body language, the odds are that communication among you and your spouse will be disturbed.

16. Notice the time you pick to talk

Wondering how to communicate more effectively in marriage? Center around the timing.

In the event that you and your wife have something important to discuss, ensure you pick the ideal opportunity to converse with them. In the event that you have nothing to discuss, the communication among you can be really upset. Assuming you decide to converse with them when they are focused on something or tired, they may not answer in the manner in which you anticipate that they should.

17. Focus on how you state your sentences

Aside from your inherent tone and body language, the manner in which you state your sentences is likewise significant. In some cases, for the absence of a superior word, we use words that can be hostile to the listener, making them hurt.

18. Try not to hurt her through your expressions

Assuming you and your wife have battled, you should not communicate in a language that makes her hurt. At the point when we are furious or harmed, we can make statements we don't mean and lament later.

19. Pay attention to comprehend her better

Ask yourself, would you say you are paying attention to comprehend or to answer? Change your methodology towards what your better half says assuming it is the last option. You will see communication getting better immediately.

20. Know when the time has come to stop

Now and then, conversations between couples can get warmed. It is vital for you to know when to delay and take your brain off the conversation. You both can continue the discussion when you are in a superior mental space.

21. Be conscious

Recollect that you and your wife are against the issue and not both of you against one another. At the point when that's what you do, you are extremely deferential towards one another. Recollect that the contention or the conversation will keep going just so lengthy, yet your marriage is until the end of time.

22. Try not to insult

Anything that you say, make an effort not to insult one another. Try not to denounce or raise fingers at one another. A sound conversation is without these things and is the main thing to make a big difference for the communication and marriage to flourish.

CHAPTER 4

Some Deadly Mistakes That Can Destroy Your Marriage

Indeed, even the most grounded of relationships have their hiccups. Sometimes, things tend to go wrong in our relationships and marriage because of our actions and inactions towards our partner. Below are some of the deadly mistakes that have the potential of damaging our marriage entirely, if care is not taken:

1. Not putting each other first

When you wed, focus on one another. This doesn't mean remaining together like paste, be that as it may. All things being equal, consider your marriage and your other commitments as an arrangement of governing rules. Assuming that you notice that your time is all spent working or pursuing the children, carve out an opportunity to ensure you really hang out with your wife. One night out with her could sound messy, yet it works.

2. Inadequate communication

When there is ineffective or poor communication between you and your spouse, confusion and misunderstanding will set it. Shouting at each other or closing down and declining to talk are similarly undesirable ways of belligerence. Figure out how to discuss frustrations without accusing each other.

3. Secrecy

Avoid being secretive all the time. You need not to tell lies in order to hide your flaws or mistakes. Try to discuss your day and stresses, guiltless as they might be. Maybe you're hesitant that you didn't get that advancement and presently feel remorseful. Couldn't you feel hurt on the off chance that your spouse lied to you, as well? Marriages are based on trust and on the off chance that you can't take ownership of easily overlooked details, it will be significantly more earnestly to get the guts to handle significant discussions.

4. Not saying 'sorry' when at a fault

We are in general grown-ups here and on the off chance that you did something wrong, or put you in a bad mood, you really need to apologize. Cultivate the habit of admitting that you are wrong and saying "I'm sorry" to please your spouse. It doesn't cost you anything to apologize.

5. Not showing appreciation

You are the type that doesn't show any iota of appreciation no matter the magnanimity of love and care that one showers on you. This is not good. Learn at least how to say "thank you". Always show appreciation for the things your companion is doing, regardless of whether they are normal or not. Appreciation goes quite far particularly when one of you is stuck accomplishing something irritating, such as finishing up tax documents. Regardless of whether your spouse appreciates cutting the grass, don't underrate the force of showing appreciation for impeccably manicured grass.

6. Applying envy

There is a major contrast between getting some information about his day and interrogating him about each second he's not with you. At the point when your partner notices that a new female staff assumed duty at his firm, you shouldn't circle back to, "Is she pretty?" We as a whole have instabilities yet reliably desirous ways of behaving and manipulative remarks make clear mileage on your relationship.

7. Evading professional assistance

Here and there dealing with marriage issues all alone doesn't work. In any case, don't tap out until you take a stab at settling your issues with an authorized marriage specialist. These are profoundly prepared experts who have seen everything and might give out professional advice as well as assist you at any point to better understand your spouse. The sooner you find support, the better.

CHAPTER 5

The Most Effective Ways To Win Your Wife Back

People and human feelings are one of the most perplexing things that occasionally get hard to comprehend. Relationships also fall under this class and many individuals decide on the foundation of marriage, feeling that all will be great and cheerful in it! Yet, that isn't true; there are numerous changes and sacrifices that one requires to make for the union to work.

Nonetheless, some of the time issues in a marriage might heighten to such an extent that the couple might choose to head out in different directions or get divorced. In the event that you have separated from your wife, yet, you can't envision your existence without her and yearning to get back with her, indeed, you can really accomplish that!

Parting ways from your better half might give you some point of view and may assist you with seeing things from an alternate perspective and assuming you are longing to return to her, these following tips could be helpful:

How To Make Your Wife Happy And Love You More

1. Communication

You might be battling or having contrasts that might turn all severe. Hence, assuming you are intending to get your wife back after she leaves you, you need to establish mature communication where no measure of pessimism holds any spot. Ladies value communication in a relationship as it assists them with laying out more transparency, empathy, genuineness, and understanding. You really have to open every one of the entryways of communication to allow your relationship another opportunity.

2. Put more efforts

Simply the way when you value something, you try to take care of it; similar to your vehicle, your home, and so, marriage is the same. You really need to put forth attempts to get back affection and sympathy into your relationship. Put forth attempts to cause her to feel extraordinary, adored, minded, and esteemed. Doing so can assist you with winning her back before it's past the point of no return!

3. Be persistent and have patience

There is a probability that you might be in a spot that she may not be in. she needs some time to heal or reconcile her conflicting thoughts within her. So, you really must give her time until she feels good to work things out with you. Being strong or fretful may negatively affect your relationship.

4. Bring the change

In some cases relationships or marriage might end up being sore and lead to separations as a result of specific missteps on your part. You genuinely should introspect and figure out what prompted such a circumstance. In the event that you are to blame, you ought to acknowledge your flaws and put forth attempts to correct them by acquiring the progressions in you. This might make your better half experience passionate feelings for you again after parting!

5. Register your assurance

In some cases, she may feel torn or harmed with a portion of the activities that might make her reluctant to get back to you. In any case, you really have to give her an assurance that the past has been forgotten and won't ever reemerge. Guarantee her that you will put forth attempts to make this relationship work and request that she put her confidence in you once more. This sort of consolation can function admirably when you wish to win back your wife after an issue!

6. Never get the past in-between

To get your ex back from another man, do whatever it takes not to discuss the past. There is no rejecting that detachment is typically a result of undesirable circumstances throughout everyday life. Move beyond it and view your relationship in another light. Try not to consider each other's missteps and attempt to safeguard who was correct or wrong. Forget about the past and turn out together for a future with the lady you are such a huge amount in love with.

7. Try not to be negative

Getting back with your wife may not be that simple and consequently there might be circumstances or conditions that might hurt you, for example, her reluctance to return, her unforgiving words about the past with you, etc. It is normal for individuals to settle on frightful words or activities when they are in dispute. During such troublesome and testing times, you ought to keep composed and be patient. Let her take as much time as necessary to feel that she can trust you once more!

8. Attempt to charm her once more

Make her become hopelessly enamored with you once more. Give her blossoms, sing tunes, compose sonnets, or do any other thing you like to do to win her back once more. Tell her the degree of your adoration and how far you can go to make things work with her. Do anything that will cause her to feel exceptional and fall head over heels for you once more.

9. Be you

Indeed, we directly or indirectly talked about making changes before in this book; however, those changes comprise correcting the slip-ups in the relationship. Nonetheless, it is basic to comprehend that to return your better half once again to you, don't roll out ridiculous improvements or responsibilities that you can't satisfy or stay aware of. Yes, you committed errors and indeed, you need her back, yet, not on the conditions that change your personality. In the excursion to get your sweetheart back in your life, don't think twice about things that you will be unable to do.

10. Never give upon her

Getting back with your wife may not come that simple and you might need to buckle down towards it by putting forth certifiable attempts. Love can recuperate all that and even assist you with prevailing upon your lost love. Be patient and reliable with your endeavors and soon you might get her covered in your life!

11. Attempt marriage mentoring

In the event that you can't resolve things with her, then you should seek professional assistance. For example, attempting marriage mentoring can be valuable. At times issues might appear to be trifling, yet, the specialists might assist you with getting a more profound viewpoint into your concerns and help you in settling them. Almost certainly, your significant other may discuss her interests and stresses with the therapist as opposed to examining them with you.

CHAPTER 6

Conclusion

Marriage is one of the most devout and hallowed relationships and assuming you bobbled in it, it doesn't imply that you fizzled and you ought to surrender. Assuming there are issues that you can deal with your spouse, it gives you sufficient motivation to attempt to get back with her. We trust a portion of the previously mentioned tips will come valuable when you attempt to work things with your wife!

Love her as you love yourself. On the off chance that you will figure out how to adore yourself by supporting it with great ideals, like persistence, honesty, generosity, empathy, grasping, dependability, and poise, you won't find it hard to likewise cherish your wife. This is on the grounds that you will do to her what you do to yourself. You will believe that your better half should encounter the delight of cherishing and being adored. You will need to try not to hurt her as you hurt yourself. In this manner, the two of you will appreciate your marriage together;

you will live together in love and harmony now and forever!

Printed in Great Britain
by Amazon